The Book of
STEAK

The Book of STEAK

Cooking for carnivores

First published 2013 by Parragon Books, Ltd.

Copyright © 2018 Cottage Door Press, LLC
5005 Newport Drive
Rolling Meadows, Illinois 60008

LOVE FOOD is an imprint of Cottage Door Press, LLC.

LOVE FOOD and the accompanying heart device are trademarks of Cottage Door Press, LLC.

10 9 8 7 6 5 4 3 2 1

ISBN: 978-1-68052-411-6

New photography by Mike Cooper
New recipes and food styling by Lincoln Jefferson
Introduction by Robin Donovan
Project managed by Alice Blackledge
Designed by Beth Kalynka

Notes for the Reader

This book uses standard kitchen measuring spoons and cups. All spoon and cup measurements are level unless otherwise indicated. Unless otherwise stated, milk is assumed to be whole, butter is assumed to be salted, eggs are large, individual vegetables are medium, and pepper is freshly ground black pepper. Unless otherwise stated, all root vegetables should be washed and peeled before using.

For the best results, use a meat thermometer when cooking meat and poultry—check the latest USDA government guidelines for current advice.

Garnishes and serving suggestions are all optional and not necessarily included in the recipe ingredients or method.

The times given are only an approximate guide. Preparation times differ according to the techniques used by different people and the cooking times may also vary from those given. Optional ingredients, variations, or serving suggestions have not been included in the calculations.

Recipes using raw or very lightly cooked eggs should be avoided by infants, the elderly, pregnant women, and people with weakened immune systems. Pregnant and breast-feeding women are advised to avoid eating peanuts and peanut products. People with nut allergies should be aware that some of the prepared ingredients used in the recipes in this book may contain nuts. Always check the packaging before use.

WHAT'S YOUR BEEF?

Whether you've decided to splurge on a fancy meal or are just craving some iron-rich beef, buying steak can seem a bit overwhelming. There's a whole lot of information that goes into making the right steak choice. The cut, of course, is important and your choice will be largely determined by your budget and how you plan to cook the meat (see our guide to cuts on pages 10–11). However, you still need to decide if you'll buy from a full-service butcher or a supermarket meat case; grass-fed or grain-fed; meat graded Prime, Choice, or Select; conventionally raised or organic. Who knew buying ingredients for dinner could involve so many decisions?

In order to make a truly informed choice about your dinner, you should be aware of a number of factors when buying a good steak—you'll never prepare a truly great steak without first having good meat to cook with.

ORGANIC

Organic beef—that is, beef that is fed only certified organic grains and grasses, never treated with growth hormones or antibiotics, and given unrestricted outdoor access— is expensive and hard to come by. The good news for consumers is that it is possible to find beef that is raised humanely, without hormones (which may increase cancer risk), antibiotics (which promote antibiotic-resistant strains of bacteria), or feed containing animal parts (which can spread bovine spongiform encephalopathy, better known as mad cow disease). Look for beef that includes a guarantee that the animals were never given antibiotics, hormones, or nonvegetarian feed.

GRASS FED

These days, grass-fed beef is showing up in the market, creating some confusion. All cows start out on a diet of grass, but conventionally raised cows are "finished" on a diet of grains for quick weight gain. Many environmentalists, animal rights advocates, and health experts argue that beef raised solely on a diet of grass is better—better for the planet because grass takes less energy to grow; better for the cows because feeding on grassy pastures is what nature intended; and better for your health because it is higher in nutrients and lower in fat.

BUYERS GUIDE

Simply put, buying from a butcher gives you the most control over all of the other choices you'll make. Not only will a butcher have plenty of cuts and very fresh meat, but being an expert, he or she will be able to help you choose wisely. If buying direct from a butcher isn't possible, be sure you're getting fresh, quality meat by checking for good, red color and taut, clear plastic wrap. Pass up any packages in which blood has pooled in the bottom, a sure sign that the meat has been sitting on the shelf for a while.

The USDA (United States Department of Agriculture) assigns all meat a grade based on quality as determined by several factors, including carcass maturity, firmness, texture, and color of lean, as well as the amount and distribution of marbling (those white flecks of fat that when well distributed throughout the muscle make a good steak tender, juicy, and flavorful). Prime is the highest grade, followed by Choice and Select. A good rule of thumb is always to buy the highest grade of meat you can afford. Of course, flavor, tenderness, and juiciness are always of the utmost importance. To be sure of a tasty steak, look for meat with consistent marbling, red blood, and nice color.

Two important points to keep in mind when choosing between grass- or grain-fed beef are flavor and fat-to-lean ratio. Grass-fed beef is more strongly flavored—some say its richer, while others are less complimentary—and it is much leaner, making it easy to overcook. In the end, your own politics, beliefs, budget, and taste will help you decide which to buy.

STORING BEEF

Most beef can be stored in the packaging it comes in at the bottom of the refrigerator for up to 3–5 days (depending on how fresh it is when you buy it), but check the expiration date, if it's provided on the packaging. Ground beef, hamburgers, and variety meats do not keep as well and should be eaten within 1–2 days.

You can freeze beef by removing the supermarket packaging and wrapping it well in freezer plastic wrap, then aluminum foil; wrap cuts individually. Freeze steaks for 6–12 months, roasts for 4– 12 months, chops 4–6 months, and ground beef, hamburgers, and variety meats 3–4 months. Frozen beef should be defrosted in the refrigerator until completely thawed. Place it in a dish or on a tray to catch any drips. Do not refreeze raw beef that has been defrosted; however, if you use the defrosted beef to make a dish that is cooked, you can freeze the cooked dish.

REFRIGERATE 1–5 DAYS
FREEZE 3–12 MONTHS

WHAT COMES FROM WHERE?

Chuck
(Chuck steaks and chuck roast)

This portion of the cow has more collagen than other parts, which gives it plenty of flavor. Because it is also quite lean, steaks cut from the chuck are best cooked using "wet" cooking methods, such as braising or marinating, to tenderize the meat before grilling. Chuck is also ideal for use as ground beef.

Rib
(Prime rib and rib-eye steaks)

These premium cuts are tender, juicy, and full of great marbling, making them perfect candidates for cooking over dry heat, such as on a barbecue or grill.

Brisket

This is tougher meat, best for braising in stews, low-and-slow barbecuing, or smoking.

Shank

The toughest cut of all, this meat is usually reserved for slow braising and stews.

Plate
(Short ribs, skirt, and hanger steaks)

Relatively tough and high in fat, meat from this part of the animal is best braised (short ribs) or tenderized in a marinade and then grilled or seared (skirt and hanger steaks).

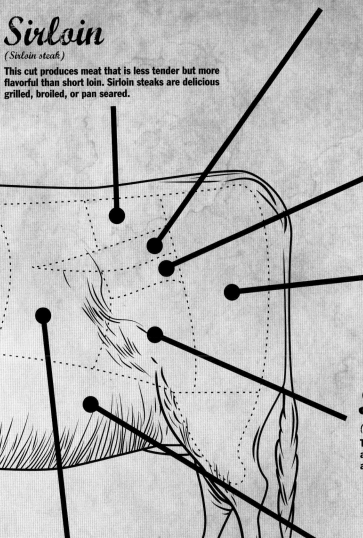

Tenderloin

(Filet mignon, tournedos, and tenderloin steaks)

This lean meat comes from a part of the cow that doesn't bear the animal's weight, making it the most tender part. These cuts are delicious no matter how you cook them—grilled, broiled, pan seared, or oven roasted.

Sirloin

(Sirloin steak)

This cut produces meat that is less tender but more flavorful than short loin. Sirloin steaks are delicious grilled, broiled, or pan seared.

Top sirloin

(Top sirloin steaks)

This lean cut has less marbling than the more prized cuts (such as those from the tenderloin), making it less tender. Still nice and flavorful, this cut is affordable and with a little pounding or marinating, makes for a tasty steak, whether grilled, broiled, or pan seared.

Round

(Top and bottom round steak and eye of round)

This portion contains meat that is lean, somewhat tough, and with little marbling. Marinating will help to tenderize the meat, as will moist cooking methods, such as braising.

Bottom sirloin

(Bottom sirloin steaks and tri-tip)

This portion is similar to top sirloin, but leaner and less tender. These cuts are best marinated and then grilled or oven roasted.

Flank

(Flank steak)

With a lot of connective tissue, this cut is tougher than premium cuts, but very flavorful. Much of the flank is used for grinding into ground beef. The flank steak is great for grilling, provided it is first well tenderized in a marinade.

Short loin

(T-bone, New York, tenderloin filet, top sirloin, Porterhouse, and strip steaks)

These well-marbled cuts produce tender, juicy, and flavorful steaks on the grill. All but the T-bone are also ideal for searing in a pan (the bone in a T-bone makes consistent pan searing difficult).

Roasting

Best used for cooking tender roasts of meat, such as rib of beef—the roast is seasoned and placed in a hot oven and cooked, basting as often as possible with the fat that renders out of it, until the meat is done to your liking. Roast beef can be served pink in the middle. Try a tasty crust for extra flavor and texture—such as the Ranch Steak with a blue cheese crust on page 24.

Slow-roast

A great way of cooking not-so-tender cuts that are too tough to roast normally. It's the same as roasting, except the oven temperature is lower, and more time is needed to break down the fibers.

Frying

Tender cuts such as steaks are often fried in oil or butter in a heavy, hot skillet, turned every now and again until they are cooked to your liking. Pair a good steak with a classic sauce, such as Béarnaise (page 54) or peppercorn (page 58) and a side of Triple-Cooked Fries (page 110).

Broiling

A good alternative to frying steak—make sure that the broiler is as hot as possible before putting the meat under it. Initially, seal under high heat, then reduce the temperature to cook through to your liking (this produces a crispy outside and juicy inside).

Poaching

Is a delicate way of cooking tender cuts of meat. Just like fish, meat can be poached in stock or wine, removed when just cooked, and served with dressings or sauces to help lift its flavor.

Stewing

Best for cooking tough cuts, such as shoulder, shank, and brisket of beef. The meat is cooked gently and slowly in a pot, either on the stove or in the oven, with vegetables, flavorings (herbs and spices), and either stock, wine, beer, or water, until it's tender enough to eat. Stewed in a sticky barbecue marinade, the Short Ribs on page 38 are the perfect example of when slower is better.

COOKING TIMES

Extra rare *(blue)* **Prepare the steak as instructed, then place in the preheated pan and seal both sides of the meat. The steak should be browned on the outside, but still raw in the middle. When pressed it should bulge slightly, and the indentation should remain in the meat.**

Rare **Prepare the steak as instructed, then place in the preheated pan and seal both sides of the meat. The steak should be warm through the middle, browned on the outside, but still pink in the center. It will be slightly more resistant to the touch than an extra-rare steak.**

*Cooking times will vary, depending on the type and thickness of the steak and how hot your pan is.

Medium Prepare the steak as instructed, then place in the preheated pan and seal both sides of the meat. The steak should be more brown than pink, but still slightly pink in the center. When pressed, a medium steak will offer some resistance and the indentation will spring back into place.

Medium rare Prepare the steak as instructed, then place in the preheated pan and seal both sides of the meat. The steak should be browned on the outside, but still slightly pink in the center. When pressed, the indentation should remain, but will quickly pool with cooking juices.

Well done Prepare the steak as instructed, then place in the preheated pan and seal both sides of the meat. The steak should be brown all the way through. When pressed, the steak will offer a good deal of resistance and will spring immediately back into place.

RIB-EYE STEAK IN A BOURBON MARINADE

Chuck Steak in a green herb marinade

22 DRUNK CHUCK STEAK IN A RICH RED WINE MARINADE

RANCH STEAK WITH A BLUE CHEESE CRUST

Beef Short Ribs with bacon and herb sauce

28 SLOW COOKED BRISKET WITH A SPICY DRY RUB

ROAST RIB OF BEEF WITH A FIERY HORSERADISH CRUST

34 Flat Iron Steak with lemon and basil pesto

SKIRT STEAK WITH BLOODY MARY BUTTER

SHORT RIBS IN A BARBECUE MARINADE

FORTY RIB-EYE STEAK WITH ROAST PEPPER SALSA

PRIME RIB WITH TRADITIONAL HORSERADISH SAUCE

CHAPTER ONE
UP FRONT CUTS

Rib-Eye Steak
in a bourbon marinade

Ingredients

FEEDS 4　　**PREP 10 mins**　　**COOK 10 mins**

4 rib-eye steaks,
12 ounces each
2 tablespoons olive oil
2 tablespoons butter

marinade
2 tablespoons extra virgin
olive oil
1 cup good quality
bourbon
1 small bunch thyme,
leaves picked
1 teaspoon dried oregano
2 garlic cloves, crushed
1 teaspoon salt
1 teaspoon pepper

1. Place all of the marinade ingredients into a shallow, nonmetallic dish that is large enough to hold all of the steaks in a single layer. Mix the ingredients together.

2. Add the steaks to the marinade, turning a few times to coat. Cover and chill in the refrigerator for a minimum of 4 hours, or for up to 12 hours if time allows. Turn once, midway through marinating.

3. Remove from the refrigerator before cooking to let the meat return to room temperature. Reserve the remaining marinade.

4. Preheat a large skillet over high heat and add the oil and butter. Cook the steaks for 5 minutes on each side for medium-rare, or until cooked to your liking. Cook the steaks in batches, if necessary. Set aside to rest for 5 minutes before serving.

5. Meanwhile, reduce the heat to medium-high, pour the reserved marinade into the skillet, and flambé to create a sauce. Serve the steaks with the sauce poured over the top.

Chuck Steak

in a green herb marinade

Ingredients

4 chuck steaks,
12 ounces each

marinade
¼ cup olive oil
1 tablespoon packed
light brown sugar
2 tablespoons red
wine vinegar
2 tablespoons chopped
flat-leaf parsley
2 tablespoons chopped
basil
2 tablespoons chopped
tarragon
2 tablespoons chopped
thyme
2 garlic cloves, crushed
1 teaspoon salt
1 teaspoon pepper

1. Place all of the marinade ingredients into a shallow, nonmetallic dish that is large enough to hold all of the steaks in a single layer. Mix the ingredients together.

2. Add the steaks to the marinade, turning a few times to coat. Cover and chill in the refrigerator for a minimum of 4 hours, or for up to 12 hours if time allows. Turn once, midway through marinating.

3. Remove from the refrigerator before cooking to let the meat return to room temperature. Discard the marinade.

4. Preheat a ridged grill pan over high heat and cook the steaks for 5 minutes on each side for medium-rare, or until cooked to your liking. Cook the steaks in batches, if necessary. Set aside to rest for 5 minutes before serving.

Acidic vinegar in the marinade helps to tenderize the steak, while the herbs give the meat a fresh, light flavor.

Drunk Chuck Steak

in a rich red wine marinade

Ingredients

FEEDS 4 · **PREP 10 mins** · **COOK 10 mins**

4 chuck steaks,
12 ounces each

marinade
¼ cup olive oil
½ cup good-quality
red wine
1 small bunch thyme,
leaves picked
1 small bunch rosemary,
leaves picked
2 garlic cloves, crushed
1 tablespoon Dijon
mustard
1 teaspoon salt
1 teaspoon pepper

1. Place all of the marinade ingredients into a shallow, nonmetallic dish that is large enough to hold all of the steaks in a single layer. Mix the ingredients together.

2. Add the steaks to the marinade, turning a few times to coat. Cover and chill in the refrigerator for a minimum of 4 hours, or for up to 12 hours if time allows. Turn once, midway through marinating.

3. Remove from the refrigerator before cooking to let the meat return to room temperature. Discard the marinade.

4. Preheat a ridged grill pan over high heat and cook the steaks for 5 minutes on each side for medium-rare, or until cooked to your liking. Cook the steaks in batches, if necessary. Set aside to rest for 5 minutes before serving.

Ranch Steak

with a blue cheese crust

Ingredients

FEEDS 4

PREP 10 mins

COOK 15 mins

4 ranch steaks or chuck shoulder steaks, 12 ounces each
1 teaspoon salt
1 teaspoon pepper
¼ cup olive oil

blue cheese crust
2 tablespoons olive oil
3 cups fresh bread crumbs
2 tablespoons chopped flat-leaf parsley
2 garlic cloves, crushed
1⅔ cups crumbled blue cheese

1. Preheat the oven to 400°F. Season the steaks with the salt and pepper, then rub with the olive oil.

2. Preheat a large skillet over high heat and seal the steaks on both sides. Transfer the steaks to a large, shallow roasting pan.

3. To make the blue cheese crust, mix together the olive oil, bread crumbs, parsley, and garlic. Sprinkle the blue cheese over the steaks, then top with the bread crumb mixture.

4. Place the steaks in the preheated oven and cook for 10–12 minutes, or until the cheese has melted and the bread crumbs have turned golden brown for medium-rare, or cover with aluminum foil and return to the oven until cooked to your liking. Remove from the oven and set aside to rest for 5 minutes before serving.

Beef Short Ribs

with bacon and herb sauce

Ingredients

4 bacon strips, cut into ½-inch pieces
3½ pounds beef short ribs
1 large onion, diced
1 celery stalk, diced
4 garlic cloves, finely chopped
2 tablespoons all-purpose flour
1 cup dry sherry
3 cups beef stock
2 teaspoons tomato paste
6 fresh thyme sprigs
1 bay leaf
salt and pepper, to taste

1. Preheat the oven to 350°F.

2. Put the bacon in a large dutch oven or flameproof casserole dish and cook over medium heat until the fat is rendered. Remove the bacon with a slotted spoon and set aside, leaving the fat in the pot.

3. Increase the heat to medium-high, add the short ribs to the dutch oven, and seal on all sides. Remove from the pot and set aside. Add the onion and celery, reduce the heat to medium, and cook for 5 minutes, or until the onion is soft.

4. Add the garlic and flour to the dutch oven and cook, stirring, for 2 minutes. Whisk in the sherry, increase the heat to high, and bring to a boil. Use a wooden spoon to scrape the sediment from the bottom of the pot. Add the stock, tomato paste, thyme, and bay leaf, and season generously with salt and pepper.

5. Add the ribs and reserved bacon, cook until simmering, then cover tightly and place in the preheated oven. Cook for 2 hours, or until the meat is tender. Skim any excess fat from the top of the cooking liquid and adjust the seasoning, if necessary. Serve with the sauce spooned over the short ribs.

These short ribs are cut "English style" (parallel to the bone) but you can also buy fattier "flanken style" (cut across the bone) and cook in the same way.

Slow Cooked Brisket

with a spicy dry rub

Ingredients

FEEDS 4–6

PREP 10 mins

COOK 3–4 hours

4½-pound boneless
brisket of beef
2 cups water

spicy dry rub
1 tablespoon dried
oregano
1 tablespoon hot smoked
paprika
1 tablespoon cumin seeds
1 teaspoon garlic salt
1 teaspoon ground
cinnamon
2 tablespoons packed
light brown sugar
1 teaspoon salt
1 teaspoon pepper

1. Preheat the oven to 325°F.

2. Place all of the dry rub ingredients in a mortar and pestle and crush to a coarse powder. Alternatively, process in a food processor or blender to achieve the desired consistency.

3. Place the brisket on a large cutting board and sprinkle with the rub mix, turning the brisket to coat. Transfer to a wire rack over a roasting pan, place in the preheated oven, and cook for 1 hour.

4. Remove from the oven and add the water to the roasting pan. Cover the pan with aluminum foil and return to the oven for an additional 2½ hours.

5. Remove from the oven and test the meat—it should be cooked through and tender. If necessary, return the pan to the oven for an additional 30 minutes. Set aside to rest for 10 minutes before serving.

Position the brisket fat-side up in the roasting pan—as the beef cooks and the fat melts, it will baste the meat.

Roast Rib of Beef

with a fiery horseradish crust

Ingredients

FEEDS 4–6   PREP 10 mins   COOK 50 mins

4½-pound rib of beef, on the bone
1 teaspoon salt
1 teaspoon pepper
¼ cup olive oil

horseradish crust
2 tablespoons extra virgin olive oil
¼ cup creamed horseradish
2 tablespoons English mustard
juice and zest of 1 lemon
½ teaspoon salt
½ teaspoon pepper

1. Preheat the oven to 350°F.

2. Place the beef rib on a large cutting board and season with the salt and pepper.

3. Place all of the horseradish crust ingredients into a small bowl and mix until combined to a rough paste.

4. Heat the olive oil in a large skillet over medium-high heat and seal the rib on all sides. Transfer to a wire rack positioned over a roasting pan and brush all over with the horseradish paste. Place the pan in the preheated oven and cook for 50 minutes.

5. Remove the rib from the oven and set aside to rest for 30 minutes before serving. Serve with the juices from the roasting pan poured over the meat.

Flat Iron Steak

with lemon and basil pesto

Ingredients

FEEDS 4   **PREP 10 mins**   **COOK 10 mins**

4 flat iron steaks,
12 ounces each
2 tablespoons olive oil
1 teaspoon salt
1 teaspoon pepper

lemon and basil pesto
2 garlic cloves, crushed
zest of 2 lemons
¾ cup pine nuts
1 cup freshly grated
Parmesan cheese
¼ cup extra virgin
olive oil
1 large bunch basil
½ teaspoon salt
1 teaspoon pepper

1. Place the steaks on a large cutting board, rub with the olive oil, and season with the salt and pepper.

2. Preheat a ridged grill pan over high heat and cook the steaks for 5 minutes on each side for medium-rare, or until cooked to your liking. Cook the steaks in batches, if necessary. Set aside to rest for 5 minutes before serving.

3. Meanwhile, place all of the pesto ingredients in a mortar and pestle and crush to a coarse paste. Alternatively, process in a food processor or blender to achieve the desired consistency. Serve the steaks with the lemon and basil pesto.

Skirt Steak

with Bloody Mary butter

FEEDS 4 | PREP 10 mins | COOK 10 mins

Ingredients

4 skirt steaks,
12 ounces each
2 tablespoons olive oil
1 teaspoon salt
1 teaspoon pepper

Bloody Mary butter
1¼ sticks unsalted butter
1 teaspoon hot sauce
1 tablespoon
Worcestershire sauce
1 tablespoon horseradish
sauce
1 large tomato, peeled,
seeded, and diced
1 teaspoon celery salt
1 teaspoon pepper

1. Place the steaks on a large cutting board, rub with the olive oil, and season with the salt and pepper.

2. Preheat a ridged grill pan over high heat and cook the steaks for 5 minutes on each side for medium-rare, or until cooked to your liking. Cook the steaks in batches, if necessary. Set aside to rest for 5 minutes before serving.

3. Meanwhile, mix all of the Bloody Mary butter ingredients together, then spoon on top of the warm steaks before serving.

Short Ribs

in a barbecue marinade

Ingredients

4½ pounds beef short ribs

marinade
1 onion, finely chopped
2 garlic cloves, crushed
2 tablespoons English mustard
1 tablespoon smoked paprika
1 tablespoon dried oregano
1 tablespoon smoked chipotle sauce
1 teaspoon fennel seeds
½ cup light soy sauce
½ cup firmly packed dark brown sugar
½ cup ketchup
½ cup cider vinegar
1 cup water
1 teaspoon celery salt
1 teaspoon pepper

1. Place all of the marinade ingredients into a large, nonmetallic bowl and mix together.

2. Add the ribs to the marinade, cover, and chill in the refrigerator for a minimum of 4 hours, or for up to 12 hours if time allows. Turn every couple of hours to coat.

3. Preheat the oven to 350°F. Place all of the ribs, with the marinade, into a large dutch oven or flameproof casserole dish with a tight fitting lid. Cover and place in the preheated oven for 3 hours.

4. Remove the dish from the oven and let cool slightly, then remove the ribs from the sauce and set aside to keep warm. Skim off any excess fat from the surface of the remaining marinade, then place the dutch oven over medium heat and reduce to a sticky consistency. Serve with the reduced barbecue marinade drizzled over the ribs.

Rib-Eye Steak

with roast pepper salsa

Ingredients

FEEDS 4 · **PREP 10 mins** · **COOK 40 mins**

4 rib-eye steaks,
12 ounces each
2 tablespoons olive oil
1 teaspoon salt
1 teaspoon pepper

roast pepper salsa
1 large red onion,
quartered
4 garlic cloves
2 red bell peppers, halved
and seeded
2 yellow bell peppers,
halved and seeded
2 tomatoes, halved
2 large red chiles,
medium heat
1 tablespoon sweet
smoked paprika
¼ cup olive oil
1 tablespoon dried
oregano
2 tablespoons sherry
vinegar
1 teaspoon salt
1 teaspoon pepper
2 tablespoons chopped
flat-leaf parsley

1. Preheat the oven to 400°F.

2. Place all of the salsa ingredients, apart from the parsley, into a large, nonmetallic mixing bowl. Mix the ingredients together, then transfer to a large shallow roasting pan. Place the pan in the preheated oven for 30 minutes, or until everything is softened and the edges of the vegetables are beginning to blacken. Once cooked, remove the roasting pan from the oven and let cool.

3. Meanwhile, place the steaks on a large cutting board, rub with the olive oil, and season with the salt and pepper.

4. Preheat a ridged grill pan over high heat and cook the steaks for 5 minutes on each side for medium-rare, or until cooked to your liking. Cook the steaks in batches, if necessary. Set aside to rest for 5 minutes before serving.

5. Place all of the roasted salsa ingredients on a cutting board with the parsley, and coarsely chop. Serve the salsa alongside the steaks.

For a slightly sweeter salsa, swap the yellow bell peppers for two handfuls of ripe cherry tomatoes, and roast as instructed.

Prime Rib

with traditional horseradish sauce

FEEDS 2 per rib **PREP** 5 mins **COOK** 2–2½ hours

Ingredients

9-pound standing rib roast, trimmed and tied
2½ tablespoons softened butter (or ½ tablespoon per rib bone)
salt and pepper, to taste

horseradish sauce
⅓ cup creamed horseradish
⅓ cup sour cream

1. To make the sauce, mix together the horseradish and sour cream in a small bowl. Cover with plastic wrap and chill until required.

2. Place the beef in a large roasting pan. Rub the entire surface of the meat with butter and season generously with salt and pepper. Let stand to reach room temperature.

3. Meanwhile, preheat the oven to 450°F. Put the meat in the preheated oven and roast for 20 minutes to seal the outside. Then reduce the oven temperature to 325°F and roast for 2 hours, until the temperature of the meat reaches 110–115°F when tested with a meat thermometer, for medium-rare.

4. Set aside to rest for 30 minutes before serving. While resting, the meat will continue to cook—for medium-rare the final internal temperature will be about 130–135°F. Slice and serve with the horseradish sauce.

Top Round Steak with beef gravy

NEW YORK STRIP STEAK WITH TARRAGON MUSHROOMS

FIFTY SIRLOIN STEAK WITH WATERCRESS BUTTER

STEAK SANDWICHES WITH MUSTARD DRESSING

Strip Steak with Béarnaise sauce

PORTERHOUSE STEAK WITH CHILI AND GARLIC RUB

58 T-BONE STEAK WITH PEPPERCORN SAUCE

STEAKHOUSE BURGERS WITH GRUYERE CHEESE

FLANK STEAK IN "THE BEST" BARBECUE MARINADE

66 Steak Medallions with beef and beer sauce

BEEF WELLINGTON

70 TOP SIRLOIN STEAK WITH A CHILI CRUST

CHAPTER
TWO
REAR CUTS

Top Round Steak

with beef gravy

**FEEDS
4–6**

**PREP
10 mins**

**COOK
45–50 mins**

Ingredients

2-pound top round steak,
2 inches thick
2 tablespoons
vegetable oil
salt and pepper, to taste

marinade
¼ cup balsamic vinegar
2 tablespoons olive oil
4 garlic cloves, crushed
½ teaspoon dried
rosemary

beef gravy
1 stick butter
½ onion, diced
½ cup all-purpose flour
1 garlic clove,
finely chopped
5 cups beef stock
2 teaspoons tomato paste
1 teaspoon Dijon mustard
1 teaspoon
Worcestershire sauce

1. To make the marinade, put all of the ingredients into a small nonmetallic bowl and whisk together. Put the steak on a plate and prick all over with a fork on both sides. Transfer to a resealable plastic food bag and pour in the marinade. Squeeze out the air, seal, and chill in the refrigerator for 12 hours.

2. To make the gravy, melt the butter in a saucepan over medium heat. Add the onion and cook until softened. Add the flour and cook, stirring, for about 5 minutes, or until the mixture is golden brown. Add the garlic and cook for 30 seconds. Gradually whisk in the stock, then add the remaining ingredients and season with salt and pepper. Bring to simmering point, then reduce the heat to low and simmer for 25 minutes, stirring occasionally. Strain into a gravy boat and keep warm until ready to serve.

3. Preheat the broiler to high. Transfer the steak to a large plate and pat dry. Rub all over with the vegetable oil and season on both sides with salt and pepper. Discard the marinade.

4. Place the steak in a shallow roasting pan and place under the preheated broiler. Broil for 7–8 minutes on each side for medium-rare, or until cooked to your liking.

5. Set aside to rest for 10 minutes before serving. Cut into thin slices against the grain and serve.

For extra depth of flavor, add a glass of red wine along with the beef stock when making the gravy.

New York Strip Steak

with tarragon mushrooms

Ingredients

FEEDS 4 **PREP 10 mins** **COOK 30–35 mins**

4 sirloin steaks,
10 ounces each
1 teaspoon salt
1 teaspoon pepper
1 tablespoon
vegetable oil
¼ cup chicken stock
1 tablespoon butter,
chilled

tarragon mushrooms
¼ cup olive oil
2 tablespoons butter
2 pounds large button
mushrooms, thickly sliced
2 garlic cloves,
finely chopped
3 tablespoons sherry
vinegar
1 tablespoon chopped
fresh tarragon
salt and pepper, to taste

1. To make the tarragon mushrooms, put the oil and butter into a large skillet over medium-high heat. Add the mushrooms and cook, stirring, for 10–15 minutes, or until browned. Stir in the garlic and cook for 2 minutes.

2. Pour in the vinegar and as soon as it starts to boil remove the skillet from the heat. Transfer the mushrooms to a bowl, add the tarragon, and season with salt and pepper. Set aside to cool. Once cooled, cover with plastic wrap and set aside.

3. Season the steaks on both sides with the salt and pepper. Heat the oil in a large skillet over high heat. Add the steaks and cook for 5–6 minutes on each side for medium-rare, or until cooked to your liking. Cook the steaks in batches, if necessary. Set aside to rest for 5 minutes before serving.

4. Add the stock to the hot skillet and use a wooden spoon to scrape the sediment from the bottom. When the stock has deglazed the skillet, add the butter and stir until melted. Add the mushrooms and stir until heated through. Taste and adjust the seasoning, if necessary. Serve the steaks with the butter and mushrooms.

Sirloin Steak

with watercress butter

Ingredients

FEEDS 4–6

PREP 5 mins

COOK 10 mins

4 sirloin steaks,
8 ounces each
4 teaspoons hot sauce
salt and pepper, to taste

watercress butter
6 tablespoons unsalted
butter, softened
¼ cup chopped
watercress

1. To make the watercress butter, place the butter in a small bowl and mix in the chopped watercress with a fork until combined. Cover with plastic wrap and chill for a minimum of 1 hour, or until required.

2. Sprinkle each steak with 1 teaspoon of the hot sauce and season generously with salt and pepper.

3. Heat a ridged grill pan over high heat and cook the steaks for 4 minutes on each side for medium-rare, or until cooked to your liking. Cook the steaks in batches, if necessary. Set aside to rest for 5 minutes before serving. Serve topped with the watercress butter.

Serve with a classic
steak side dish—
Triple-Cooked Fries
(see page 110).

Steak Sandwiches

with mustard dressing

Ingredients

FEEDS 4 **PREP 10 mins** **COOK 25 mins**

8 slices thick white bread
butter, softened, for
spreading
2 handfuls mixed
salad greens
3 tablespoons olive oil
2 onions, thinly sliced
1½-pound top sirloin
steak, 1 inch thick
1 tablespoon
Worcestershire sauce
2 tablespoons
whole-grain mustard
2 tablespoons water
salt and pepper, to taste

1. Spread each slice of bread with some butter and add a few salad greens to the four bottom slices.

2. Heat 2 tablespoons of the oil in a large skillet over medium heat. Add the onions and cook, stirring occasionally, for 10–15 minutes, or until softened and golden brown. Using a slotted spoon, transfer to a plate and set aside.

3. Increase the heat to high and add the remaining oil to the skillet. Add the steak, season with pepper, and seal on both sides. Reduce the heat to medium and cook for 2½–3 minutes on each side for rare, or until cooked to your liking. Transfer the steak to the plate with the onions.

4. Add the Worcestershire sauce, mustard, and water to the skillet. Use a wooden spoon to scrape the sediment from the bottom. When the liquid has deglazed the skillet, add the onions and stir. Season with salt and pepper.

5. Thinly slice the steak across the grain, divide among the four bottom slices of bread, and cover with the onions and mustard dressing. Cover with the top slices of bread and press down gently. Serve immediately.

Strip Steak

with Béarnaise sauce

Ingredients

FEEDS 4 **PREP 15 mins** **COOK 30–35 mins**

4 strip steaks,
8 ounces each
1 tablespoon olive oil
salt and pepper, to taste

Béarnaise sauce
1 large bunch tarragon
1 shallot, finely chopped
½ cup white wine vinegar
4 peppercorns
2 egg yolks
1¾ sticks butter, cubed

1. To make the Béarnaise sauce, remove the most tender leaves of the tarragon, finely chop, and set aside. Coarsely chop the remaining tarragon and add to a small saucepan with the shallot, vinegar, and peppercorns and simmer until it has reduced to about 1 tablespoon. Strain this through a strainer into a clean heatproof bowl.

2. Bring a separate small saucepan of water to the boil, place the bowl containing the vinegar reduction on top, and gently whisk in the egg yolks until the mixture thickens a little. Add the butter, a piece at a time, and whisk until the sauce is thick. Add the reserved tarragon leaves, stir, and season with salt. Remove from the heat and cover to keep warm while you cook the steaks.

3. Season the steaks with salt and pepper and rub with the oil. Heat a large skillet over high heat and add the steaks. Cook for 3–4 minutes on each side for medium-rare, or until cooked to your liking. Set aside to rest for 5 minutes before serving with the sauce.

Porterhouse Steak

with chili and garlic rub

Ingredients

FEEDS 4   **PREP** 10 mins   **COOK** 10 mins

4 porterhouse or T-bone steaks, 12 ounces each

chili and garlic rub
1 teaspoon salt
2 teaspoons pepper
¼ cup olive oil
3 garlic cloves, crushed
1 teaspoon crushed red pepper flakes

1. Place all of the chili and garlic rub ingredients in a mortar and pestle and crush to a coarse paste. Alternatively, process in a food processor or blender to achieve the desired consistency.

2. Rub the chili and garlic mixture all over the steaks.

3. Preheat a ridged grill pan over medium-high heat and cook the steaks for 5 minutes on each side for medium-rare, or until cooked to your liking. Cook the steaks in batches, if necessary. Set aside to rest for 5 minutes before serving.

T-Bone Steak

with peppercorn sauce

Ingredients

FEEDS 4 **PREP 10 mins** **COOK 20 mins**

4 T-bone steaks,
12 ounces each
1 teaspoon salt
1 teaspoon pepper
2 tablespoons olive oil

peppercorn sauce
1 tablespoon olive oil
1 tablespoon butter
2 shallots, finely chopped
2 garlic cloves, crushed
½ cup brandy
1 cup heavy cream
1 tablespoon Dijon
mustard
1 teaspoon salt
1 tablespoon mixed
cracked peppercorns

1. To make the peppercorn sauce, heat a saucepan over medium-low heat, add the oil and butter, then add the shallots and garlic and sauté for 5–10 minutes, or until translucent. Add the brandy and flambé. Add the cream and cook until reduced by half, then add the mustard, salt, and cracked peppercorns. Set aside and keep warm.

2. Season the steaks with the salt and pepper, and rub with olive oil.

3. Preheat a ridged grill pan over high heat and cook the steaks for 5 minutes on each side for medium-rare, or until cooked to your liking. Cook the steaks in batches, if necessary. Set aside to rest for 5 minutes before serving with the peppercorn sauce.

Steakhouse Burgers

with Gruyère cheese

Ingredients

1 pound boneless
chuck shoulder
1 teaspoon salt
½ teaspoon pepper
4 burger buns, split
4 slices Gruyère cheese
or Swiss cheese

1. Chop the beef into 1-inch cubes, then place on a plate, wrap in plastic wrap, and chill in the refrigerator for 30 minutes.

2. Place half the beef in a food processor or blender. Pulse (do not run the processor) about 15 times. Season the meat with half the salt and half the pepper, and pulse an additional 10–15 times until the meat is finely chopped; do not overprocess. Remove from the processor and repeat with the remaining beef. Divide into four equal portions and shape each portion into a patty.

3. Heat a ridged grill pan over medium-high heat. Add the patties and cook for 3 minutes on each side for medium-rare, or until cooked to your liking. Place a slice of cheese on top of each burger during the last 2 minutes of cooking.

4. Serve immediately, in burger buns with your preferred condiments and sides.

Make the patties in advance, wrap in wax paper and aluminum foil, and keep in the refrigerator for 1-2 days.

Flank Steak

in "the best" barbecue marinade

FEEDS
4–6

PREP
5 mins

COOK
10–15 mins

Ingredients

4 garlic cloves,
finely chopped
¼ cup olive oil,
plus extra for brushing
¼ cup firmly packed light
brown sugar
2 tablespoons red
wine vinegar
¼ cup soy sauce
1 teaspoon Dijon mustard
1 teaspoon pepper
1¾-pound whole flank
steak, trimmed
salt, to taste

1. Put all the ingredients, except the steak and salt, into a large, resealable plastic food bag. Seal and shake to combine. Add the steak and reseal the bag, squeezing out most of the air. Chill in the refrigerator for a minimum of 6 hours, or for up to 12 hours if time allows. Remove from the refrigerator before cooking to let the meat return to room temperature.

2. Transfer the steak to a large plate, reserving the remaining marinade. Pat the steak dry with paper towels and season generously on both sides with salt.

3. Heat a ridged grill pan over high heat. Brush a little oil over the surface of the pan and add the steak. Cook for 5–6 minutes on each side for medium-rare, or until cooked to your liking. Set aside to rest for 10 minutes before serving.

4. Meanwhile, pour the marinade into a small saucepan and bring to a boil. Serve the steak sliced across the grain, with the marinade on the side.

Steak Medallions

with beef and beer sauce

Ingredients

3¼-pound beef tenderloin
1 teaspoon salt
1 teaspoon pepper
2 tablespoons olive oil

beef and beer sauce
2 tablespoons olive oil
2 tablespoons butter
2 shallots, finely chopped
2 garlic cloves, crushed
2 tablespoons flour
1¼ cups beer
1¼ cups hot beef stock
2 tablespoons
Worcestershire sauce
1 tablespoon chopped
thyme
1 tablespoon chopped
parsley
1 teaspoon salt
1 teaspoon pepper

1. To make the beef and beer sauce, place a saucepan over medium heat, add the olive oil and butter, and sauté the shallots and garlic for 5–10 minutes, or until translucent. Then add the flour and cook for a few minutes, until the flour is beginning to brown. Gradually whisk in the beer, then add the beef stock and Worcestershire sauce. Reduce the sauce until it is the consistency of heavy cream, then add the thyme, parsley, and salt and pepper. Set aside and keep warm.

2. On a cutting board, season the beef tenderloin with the salt, pepper, and olive oil.

3. Preheat a ridged grill pan over medium-high heat and cook the beef tenderloin for 15–20 minutes, making sure that all sides are sealed. Set aside to rest for 10 minutes before serving, then slice and serve with the beer sauce.

Use a regular beer or a dark microbrewery beer, as preferred, to make the sauce.

Beef Wellington

Ingredients

FEEDS 4–6 **PREP 30 mins** **COOK 1 hour**

2 tablespoons olive oil
3¼-pound beef tenderloin, trimmed
4 tablespoons butter
2 cups finely chopped mushrooms
2 garlic cloves, crushed
6 ounces smooth liver pâté
1 tablespoon finely chopped fresh parsley
2 teaspoons English mustard
1 sheet ready-to-bake puff pastry, thawed if frozen
1 egg, lightly beaten
salt and pepper, to taste

1. Place a large skillet over high heat and add the olive oil. Rub salt and pepper into the beef and seal on all sides for rare. Set aside to cool.

2. Heat the butter in a skillet over medium heat, add the mushrooms, and sauté for 5 minutes. Reduce the heat, add the garlic, and cook for another 5 minutes. Put the mushrooms and garlic in a bowl, add the pâté and parsley, and mix together with a fork. Let cool.

3. Rub the mustard into the beef tenderloin. Roll out the pastry into a rectangle large enough to wrap the whole beef with some extra. Spread the mushroom paste in the middle of the pastry, leaving a 2-inch gap between the paste and the edge of the pastry, and lay the beef on top. Brush the edges of the pastry with beaten egg and fold it over, edges overlapping, and across the meat to completely enclose it.

4. Preheat the oven to 425°F. Place the wrapped beef in a roasting pan with the pastry seam underneath and brush the surface with beaten egg. Place in the refrigerator for 15 minutes to chill, then transfer to the preheated oven and bake for 50 minutes. Check on the pastry after 30 minutes; if it is golden brown, cover with aluminum foil to prevent it from burning. Set aside to rest for 15 minutes before serving.

For well-done beef, roast at 425°F for 20 minutes after sealing the meat in the skillet.

Top Sirloin Steak

with a chili crust

Ingredients

FEEDS 4–6 **PREP 10 mins** **COOK 20 mins**

4½-pound top sirloin steak

chili crust
3 tablespoons chipotle chili paste
1 teaspoon crushed red pepper flakes
3 tablespoons packed light brown sugar
3 tablespoons sherry vinegar
¼ cup olive oil
3 garlic cloves, crushed
2 teaspoons salt
2 teaspoons pepper

1. Place all of the crust ingredients in a mortar and pestle and crush to a fine paste. Alternatively, process in a food processor or blender to achieve the desired consistency.

2. Place the steak in a shallow, nonmetallic dish and cover in the chili crust, turning a few times to coat. Cover and chill in the refrigerator for a minimum of 4 hours, or for up to 12 hours if time allows.

3. Remove from the refrigerator before cooking to let the meat return to room temperature.

4. Preheat a ridged grill pan over medium-high heat and cook for 10 minutes on each side for medium-rare, or until cooked to your liking. Set the steak aside to rest for 5 minutes before serving. Slice before serving.

SEVENTY FOUR BEEF CARPACCIO

STEAK TARTARE

Top Sirloin Steak in a lemon-thyme marinade

82 SIRLOIN STEAK WITH SESAME AND SPICY ASIAN GREENS

STEAK STRIPS WITH A CHILI CRUST AND CUCUMBER DIP

Sirloin Steak in a lime and tequila marinade

SICHUAN STEAK WITH NOODLE AND RADISH SALAD 88

NINETY STUFFED STEAK WITH GOAT CHEESE AND MINT COUSCOUS

SESAME STEAK IN A GINGER MARINADE AND SOY SAUCE BROTH

Tri-Tip Steak in an Asian-spiced marinade

FLAT IRON STEAK IN A ROSEMARY AND RED WINE MARINADE

STEAK FOR TWO

Beef Carpaccio

Ingredients

FEEDS 2

PREP 5 mins

8 ounces top-quality beef tenderloin (cut from the rump end)
½ cup virgin olive oil
3 tablespoons pine nuts
5 cups arugula
¼ ounce Parmesan cheese
1 teaspoon truffle oil (optional)
salt and pepper, to taste

1. Put the beef in the freezer for 1 hour before use, so it is firm. Trim any fat or sinew from the beef, then cut the meat into slices as thinly as possible.

2. Lay a slice of beef on a cutting board and, using a flat, broad knife, press against the meat, pushing down hard and pulling across the beef in a spreading motion. Repeat with all the beef slices.

3. Pour a little pool of olive oil into a wide dish. Place a layer of beef on the oil, season lightly with salt and pepper, and pour over some more olive oil. Repeat until all the beef has been seasoned in this way. Cover and chill in the refrigerator for at least 30 minutes, or for up to 2 hours if time allows. Meanwhile, toast the pine nuts in a dry skillet over medium heat until lightly browned and set aside.

4. Pile a bed of arugula onto the serving plates, remove the beef slices from the oil, and divide evenly between the plates. Sprinkle with the pine nuts and shave the Parmesan cheese over the top, using a vegetable peeler. Drizzle with a few drops of truffle oil, if using, and serve.

Steak Tartare

Ingredients

FEEDS 2

PREP 15 mins

8 ounces top-quality beef tenderloin or sirloin steak
1 tablespoon finely chopped parsley
1 tablespoon finely chopped capers
1 tablespoon finely chopped shallots
1 tablespoon finely chopped pickles
2 dashes hot sauce
2 dashes Worcestershire sauce
1 tablespoon Dijon mustard
½ teaspoon salt
2 egg yolks (kept separate)

1. Chill all the ingredients, a cutting board, and mixing bowl for 20 minutes before you begin. Then remove from the refrigerator and finely chop the steak until minced.

2. Place the minced steak in the chilled bowl. Add all the remaining ingredients, except the egg yolks, and mix them into the beef with a fork.

3. Shape the mixture into two round patties and make an indent in the middle of each. Place in the refrigerator until ready to serve. To serve, place each patty in the middle of a plate and lay an egg yolk in the indent.

Serve with a lightly poached egg (still runny in the middle), if preferred.

Top Sirloin Steak

in a lemon–thyme marinade

Ingredients

FEEDS 2 **PREP 10 mins** **COOK 10 mins**

2 top sirloin steaks,
10 ounces each
2 tablespoons extra virgin
olive oil
juice and zest of 1 lemon
1 small bunch thyme,
leaves picked

marinade
¼ cup olive oil
1 small bunch thyme,
leaves picked
2 garlic cloves, crushed
juice and zest of 1 lemon
1 teaspoon salt
1 teaspoon pepper

1. Place all of the marinade ingredients into a shallow, nonmetallic dish that is large enough to hold both of the steaks in a single layer. Mix the ingredients together.

2. Add the steaks to the marinade, turning a few times to coat. Cover and chill in the refrigerator for a minimum of 4 hours, or for up to 12 hours if time allows. Turn once, midway through marinating. Remove from the refrigerator before cooking to let the meat return to room temperature.

3. Preheat a ridged grill pan over high heat and cook the steaks for 5 minutes on each side for medium-rare, or until cooked to your liking. Set aside to rest for 5 minutes before serving.

4. Once rested, slice the steaks, drizzle with the olive oil and lemon juice, and sprinkle with the lemon zest and thyme leaves before serving.

Sirloin Steak

with sesame and spicy Asian greens

FEEDS 2 · **PREP 15 mins** · **COOK 15 mins**

Ingredients

2 sirloin steaks,
10 ounces each
1 tablespoon olive oil
1 tablespoon sesame oil
1 tablespoon light soy sauce
2 teaspoons toasted
sesame seeds
1 teaspoon pepper

spicy Asian greens
1 tablespoon olive oil
2 garlic cloves,
finely chopped
¾-inch piece ginger, finely
chopped
1 small red chile, finely
chopped
2 scallions, finely sliced
1 pound Asian greens
(such as Chinese broccoli
and bok choy), trimmed
2 tablespoons light
soy sauce
1 tablespoon sesame seeds

1. Season the steaks with the olive oil, sesame oil, soy sauce, sesame seeds, and pepper.

2. Preheat a large skillet over medium-high heat and cook the steaks for 5 minutes on each side for medium-rare, or until cooked to your liking. Set aside to rest for 5 minutes before serving.

3. Meanwhile, return the skillet to the heat. Add the olive oil, garlic, ginger, chile, scallions, and Asian greens and stir-fry until the greens begin to wilt. Add the soy sauce and sesame seeds, and serve immediately with the steak.

Steak Strips

with a chili crust and cucumber dip

Ingredients

vegetable oil, for
deep-frying

steak strips
2 tablespoons all-purpose
flour
2 eggs, beaten
1¾ cups panko bread
crumbs
1 teaspoon crushed red
pepper flakes
1 teaspoon paprika
1 teaspoon salt
1 teaspoon pepper
12 ounces beef
tenderloin, cut into strips

cucumber dip
1 cup plain yogurt
½ cucumber, grated
small bunch mint,
chopped
juice and zest of 1 lemon
1 shallot, finely chopped
salt and pepper, to taste
pinch of smoked paprika,
to garnish

1. To make the steak strips, place the flour, eggs, and bread crumbs into three separate shallow dishes. Season the bread crumbs with the red pepper flakes, paprika, salt, and pepper. Dust each steak strip in the flour, then dip in the eggs and then coat in bread crumbs and set aside.

2. Heat enough oil for deep-frying in a large saucepan or deep fryer to 350–375°F, or until a cube of bread browns in 30 seconds.

3. Meanwhile, to make the cucumber dip, mix together all of the ingredients, apart from the paprika, in a small bowl. Cover and chill in the refrigerator until required.

4. Cook the beef strips in the oil in batches, for 8–10 minutes or until golden brown, then drain on paper towels and serve with the cucumber dip sprinkled with the paprika.

Sirloin Steak

in a lime and tequila marinade

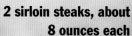

FEEDS 2 **PREP 10 mins** **COOK 10 mins**

2 sirloin steaks, about 8 ounces each

marinade
1 tablespoon olive oil
1½ tablespoons tequila
1½ tablespoons freshly squeezed orange juice
½ tablespoon freshly squeezed lime juice
2 garlic cloves, crushed
1 teaspoon chili powder
1 teaspoon ground cumin
½ teaspoon dried oregano
salt and pepper, to taste

1. Place all of the marinade ingredients into a shallow, nonmetallic dish that is large enough to hold both of the steaks in a single layer. Mix the ingredients together.

2. Add the steaks to the marinade, turning a few times to coat. Cover and chill in the refrigerator for a minimum of 2 hours, or for up to 12 hours if time allows. Turn once, midway through marinating.

3. Remove from the refrigerator before cooking, to let the meat return to room temperature. Reserve the remaining marinade.

4. Preheat a ridged grill pan over high heat and cook the steaks for 3–4 minutes on each side for medium-rare, or until cooked to your liking. Baste frequently with the remaining marinade. Set the steak aside to rest for 5 minutes before serving.

This marinade is perfect for making a quick corn relish—make a second batch and stir in canned corn kernels, chopped red bell pepper, and fresh cilantro.

Sichuan Steak

with noodle and radish salad

Ingredients

FEEDS 2

PREP 5 mins

COOK 10 mins

6 ounces sirloin steak
2 ounces dried egg noodles
½ small red onion, thinly sliced
3 radishes, sliced
2 handfuls of mustard greens, tatsoi, and arugula
1 tablespoon peanut oil
½ teaspoon Sichuan pepper

marinade
2 teaspoons Chinese rice wine
1 teaspoon soy sauce
2 teaspoons sugar
1 tablespoon hoisin sauce
½-inch piece fresh ginger, grated

dressing
1 teaspoon Sichuan pepper
1 tablespoon light soy sauce
1 tablespoon rice vinegar
1 tablespoon sesame oil

1. Place all of the marinade ingredients into a shallow, nonmetallic dish that is large enough to hold the steak in a single layer. Mix the ingredients together.

2. Trim any fat from the steak. Slice into thin strips and add to the marinade, turning a few times to coat. Cover and chill in the refrigerator for 30 minutes. Remove from the refrigerator before cooking to let the meat return to room temperature.

3. Cook the noodles in a saucepan of boiling water according to the package directions, until tender. Drain and let cool. Snip into shorter lengths using kitchen scissors and set aside.

4. Place all of the dressing ingredients into a small bowl and whisk until well blended. Combine the noodles, onion, radishes, and leafy greens in a large bowl. Pour two-thirds of the dressing over the salad. Toss to distribute the noodles, then divide between individual serving plates.

5. Heat a wok over medium-high heat, then add the peanut oil and Sichuan pepper. Stir for a few seconds to flavor the oil. Add the steak and marinade, and stir-fry for 4–5 minutes until caramelized. Remove with a slotted spoon and sprinkle over the salad. Pour the remaining dressing over the top and serve immediately.

Sichuan pepper has a numbing effect on the tongue and creates a slight tingling sensation.

Stuffed Steak

with goat cheese and mint couscous

Ingredients

FEEDS 2

PREP 20 mins

COOK 15 mins

2 sirloin steaks,
10 ounces each
1 tablespoon olive oil
salt and pepper, to taste

goat cheese stuffing
1 garlic clove, crushed
1 (4-ounce) package soft
goat cheese, chopped
6 cherry tomatoes,
chopped
2 tablespoons chopped
flat-leaf parsley
1 tablespoon olive oil
½ teaspoon pepper
½ teaspoon salt

mint couscous
½ cup couscous
1 tablespoon extra virgin
olive oil
small bunch flat-leaf
parsley, chopped
small bunch mint,
chopped
juice and zest of 1 lemon
1 shallot, finely chopped
1 large tomato, chopped

1. To make the goat cheese stuffing, place all of the ingredients into a small, nonmetallic bowl and mix well. Set aside.

2. On a cutting board, season the steaks generously with salt and pepper and rub with olive oil. With a sharp knife, cut a slit in the nonfatty side of the steaks to create a pocket (do not cut through the whole steak). Fill the pockets with the stuffing mixture and set aside.

3. To make the couscous, place the couscous and olive oil in a small, heatproof bowl and cover with boiling water. Cover the bowl with plastic wrap and let stand for 2 minutes. Remove the plastic wrap and break up the grains with a fork until light and fluffy. Add the remaining ingredients, season with salt and pepper, mix well, and set aside.

4. Preheat a ridged grill pan over medium-high heat and cook the steaks for 5 minutes on each side for medium, or until cooked to your liking. Set the steaks aside to rest for 5 minutes before serving with the couscous.

Sesame Steak

in a ginger marinade and soy sauce broth

Ingredients

FEEDS 2   **PREP 15 mins**   **COOK 25 mins**

8 ounces sirloin steak
peanut oil, for deep-frying
¼ teaspoon toasted
sesame oil
½ teaspoon chili oil
(optional)
1 teaspoon sesame
seeds, to garnish

marinade
½-inch piece fresh ginger,
thinly sliced
1 scallion, cut into
2–3 pieces
1 teaspoon rice wine
1 teaspoon toasted
sesame oil

soy sauce broth
½ cup beef stock
½ teaspoon soy sauce
½ teaspoon rice wine or
dry sherry
pinch of salt
1 teaspoon sugar
½ teaspoon fennel seeds,
crushed
½-inch piece cinnamon
stick

1. Slice the steak into thin strips and flatten with a meat mallet.

2. Place all of the marinade ingredients into a shallow, nonmetallic dish that is large enough to hold all of the steak strips in a single layer. Mix the ingredients together.

3. Add the steak to the marinade, turning a few times to coat. Cover and chill in the refrigerator for 30 minutes. Remove from the refrigerator before cooking to let the meat return to room temperature. Remove and discard the ginger and scallion.

4. Heat enough peanut oil for deep-frying in a large wok to 350–375°F, or until a cube of bread browns in 30 seconds. Add the steak strips to the wok and fry for 1 minute, stirring occasionally. Remove with a slotted spoon and drain on paper towels.

5. Return the oil temperature to 350°F. Return the meat to the wok and fry for an additional 2–3 minutes, until the strips are crisp and dark brown. Remove and drain again.

6. To make the broth, bring the stock to a boil in a separate saucepan. Add the remaining ingredients and simmer for 1 minute, then add the steak strips. Simmer over gentle heat for 15–20 minutes, stirring from time to time, until the liquid has evaporated and the meat is sticky. Remove and discard the cinnamon stick. Stir in the sesame oil and the chili oil, if using. Sprinkle with the sesame seeds and serve warm.

Appetizingly chewy, these beef slivers make a great snack or nibble to serve with drinks.

Tri-Tip Steak

in an Asian-spiced marinade

Ingredients

FEEDS
2

PREP
10 mins

COOK
10 mins

2 tri-tip or bottom sirloin
steaks, 10 ounces each

marinade
1 tablespoon olive oil
1 tablespoon sesame oil
1 teaspoon white sugar
1 tablespoon Chinese
black vinegar
¾-inch piece fresh
ginger, peeled and finely
chopped
1 garlic clove, crushed
1 tablespoon toasted
sesame seeds
1 tablespoon light
soy sauce
1 teaspoon pepper

1. Place all of the marinade ingredients into a shallow, nonmetallic dish that is large enough to hold both of the steaks in a single layer. Mix the ingredients together.

2. Add the steaks to the marinade, turning a few times to coat. Cover and chill in the refrigerator for a minimum of 4 hours, or for up to 12 hours if time allows. Turn once, midway through marinating. Remove from the refrigerator before cooking to let the meat return to room temperature. Discard the marinade.

3. Preheat a ridged grill pan over high heat and cook the steaks for 5 minutes on each side for medium-rare, or until cooked to your liking. Set the steaks aside to rest for 5 minutes before serving.

Flat Iron Steak

in a rosemary and red wine marinade

Ingredients

FEEDS 2 · **PREP 10 mins** · **COOK 10 mins**

2 flat iron steaks,
10 ounces each
1 tablespoon olive oil
1 tablespoon butter

marinade
2 tablespoons extra virgin
olive oil
1 cup good-quality
red wine
1 small bunch thyme,
leaves picked
1 small bunch rosemary,
leaves picked
2 garlic cloves, crushed
1 teaspoon salt
1 teaspoon pepper

1. Place all of the marinade ingredients into a shallow, nonmetallic dish that is large enough to hold both of the steaks in a single layer. Mix the ingredients together.

2. Add the steaks to the marinade, turning a few times to coat. Cover and chill in the refrigerator for a minimum of 4 hours, or for up to 12 hours if time allows. Turn once, midway through marinating.

3. Remove from the refrigerator before cooking to let the meat return to room temperature. Reserve the remaining marinade.

4. Preheat a large skillet over medium-high heat and add the oil and butter. Cook the steaks for 5 minutes on each side for medium-rare, or until cooked to your liking. Set the steak aside to rest for 5 minutes before serving.

5. Meanwhile, add the remaining marinade to the skillet and cook until reduced by half. Serve the steaks with the red wine marinade poured over the top.

HASH BROWNS ONE HUNDRED

MACARONI AND CHEESE

104 Creamed Spinach

106 HOMEMADE MUSTARD 107 MAYONNAISE

OOOOOONION RINGS

TRIPLE-COOKED FRIES
TRIPLE-COOKED FRIES
TRIPLE-COOKED FRIES 110

CORN ON THE COB WITH BLUE CHEESE DIP

KETCHUP 114 BARBECUE SAUCE 115

116 Scalloped Potatoes

BAKED CAULIFLOWER

122 Coleslaw NEW POTATOES WITH GARLIC AND CHILI BUTTER

SAUCES AND SIDES

Hash Browns

Ingredients

FEEDS 4 **PREP 10 mins** **COOK 40 mins**

8 russet or Yukon gold potatoes
2 tablespoons olive oil
1 large onion, sliced
1 egg, beaten
¾ cup instant mashed potatoes
vegetable oil, for deep-frying
salt and pepper, to taste

1. Place the potatoes in a large saucepan of lukewarm, salted water. Bring the water to a boil, and when the water reaches boiling point, remove the pan from the heat and let cool.

2. Heat the olive oil over low heat in a skillet. Add the onions and sauté for 5–7 minutes, until soft and translucent but not browned.

3. Once the potatoes are cool enough to handle, coarsely shred them into a large bowl. Add the sautéed onions, egg, and instant potatoes. Mix well and season with salt and pepper.

4. Heat enough oil for deep-frying in a large saucepan or deep fryer to 350–375°F, or until a cube of bread browns in 30 seconds.

5. Meanwhile, roll the potato mixture into walnut-size balls and flatten each into a patty shape. Fry, in batches, in the preheated oil until golden and let drain on paper towels before serving.

Macaroni and Cheese

 Ingredients
 FEEDS 4
 PREP 10 mins
 COOK 40 mins

8 ounces dried
macaroni pasta
2½ cups milk
½ teaspoon grated
nutmeg
4 tablespoons butter
½ cup all-purpose flour
1¾ cups shredded
cheddar cheese
½ cup grated Parmesan
cheese
salt and pepper, to taste

1. Preheat the oven to 350°F. Bring a large saucepan of lightly salted water to a boil. Add the pasta and cook according to the package directions, until tender but still firm to the bite. Remove from the heat, drain, and set aside.

2. Meanwhile, put the milk and nutmeg into a saucepan over low heat and heat until warm, but do not bring to a boil.

3. Melt the butter in a heavy saucepan over low heat, then add the flour and stir to make a paste. Cook gently for 2 minutes. Add the hot milk a little at a time, whisking it into the paste, then cook for about 10–15 minutes to make a loose sauce.

4. Add 1¼ cups of the cheddar cheese and all the Parmesan cheese and stir through until they have melted. Season with salt and pepper and remove from the heat.

5. Put the macaroni into a shallow, heatproof dish, then pour the sauce over the top. Sprinkle with the remaining cheddar cheese, place the dish in the preheated oven, and bake for about 25 minutes, until hot.

For a crisp topping, sprinkle ½ cup of fresh bread crumbs over the top with the cheese, and broil for a few minutes after baking.

Creamed Spinach

 FEEDS 4
 PREP 5 mins
 COOK 5 mins

1 tablespoon butter
3 (12-ounce) packages fresh, young spinach leaves
¼ cup light cream
½ teaspoon freshly grated nutmeg
salt and pepper, to taste

1. Melt the butter in a large skillet, add the spinach, and cook, stirring, until the leaves are wilted.

2. Continue to cook over medium heat, stirring occasionally, until most of the liquid has evaporated.

3. Stir in the cream and nutmeg, then season with salt and pepper. Serve immediately.

Swap the light cream for Greek yogurt for a healthier version of this classic side dish.

Homemade Mustard

MAKES
3/4 CUP

PREP
15 mins

Ingredients

3 tablespoons brown
mustard seeds
3 tablespoons cider
vinegar
1–2 tablespoons water
3 tablespoons dry
mustard
2 teaspoons salt
2 teaspoons honey

1. Put the mustard seeds into a small, nonmetallic container with the vinegar and enough water to cover completely. Set aside for two days, covered, at room temperature.

2. Strain the mustard seeds, reserving the liquid. Place the mustard seeds into a mortar and pestle and crush to a coarse paste—the finer the paste, the spicier the mustard will be.

3. Place the crushed mustard seeds into a small bowl with the dry mustard, salt, and honey. Add the reserved vinegar water and stir.

4. Place in a sterilized jar, seal, and refrigerate for at least two days before serving. Once opened, store in the refrigerator and consume within two weeks.

Mayonnaise

Ingredients

2 extra-large egg yolks
2 teaspoons Dijon mustard
¾ teaspoon salt, or to taste
white pepper, to taste
2–3 tablespoons lemon juice
1¼ cups sunflower oil

1. Mix the egg yolks with the Dijon mustard, salt, and white pepper in a food processor or blender. Add 2 tablespoons lemon juice and process again.

2. With the processor still running, add the oil, drop by drop at first. When the sauce begins to thicken, add the oil in a slow, steady stream. If the mayonnaise becomes too thick, add another 1 tablespoon of lemon juice.

3. Place in a sterilized jar, seal, and refrigerate. Store in the refrigerator and consume within three days.

Onion Rings

Ingredients

FEEDS 4 · **PREP 15 mins** · **COOK 15 mins**

1 cup all-purpose flour
pinch of salt
1 egg
⅔ cup low-fat milk
4 large onions
vegetable oil, for
deep-frying
salt and pepper, to taste

1. To make the batter, sift the flour and salt into a large bowl and make a well in the center. Break the egg into the well and gently beat with a whisk. Gradually whisk in the milk, drawing the flour from the sides of the bowl into the liquid in the center to form a smooth batter.

2. Leaving the onions whole, slice widthwise into ¼-inch slices, then separate each slice into rings.

3. Heat the oil in a deep fryer or deep, heavy saucepan to 350–375°F, or until a cube of bread browns in 30 seconds.

4. Using the tines of a fork, pick up several onions rings at a time and dip in the batter. Let any excess batter drip off, then add the onions to the oil and deep-fry for 1–2 minutes, until they rise to the surface of the oil and become crisp and golden brown. Remove from the oil, drain on paper towels, and keep warm while deep-frying the remaining onion rings in batches.

5. Season the onion rings with salt and pepper. Serve immediately.

Triple-Cooked Fries

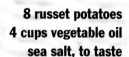

FEEDS 4 PREP 10 mins COOK 15 mins

8 russet potatoes
4 cups vegetable oil
sea salt, to taste

1. Cut the potatoes into ¼ x ¼-inch sticks. Soak the cut potatoes in a bowl of cold water for 5 minutes, then drain and rinse.

2. Bring a medium saucepan of lightly salted water to a boil over high heat. Add the potatoes, bring back to a boil, and cook for 3–4 minutes, until the potatoes begin to soften. Drain the potatoes and spread on a baking sheet lined with paper towels. Refrigerate for a minimum of 1 hour, or for up to 12 hours if time allows.

3. Place the oil in a large, heavy saucepan or a deep fryer. Heat the oil to 350–375°F, or until a cube of bread browns in 30 seconds. Carefully add the cut potatoes, in batches, if necessary, to avoid overcrowding. Cook for 3–4 minutes, until beginning to brown. Remove using tongs and drain on a plate lined with paper towels.

4. Return the oil to 350–375°F, then add the potatoes again and fry for 3–5 minutes, until golden brown and crisp. Remove from the oil and drain on a plate lined with paper towels. Season generously with sea salt and serve immediately.

Corn on the Cob

with blue cheese dip

FEEDS 6   PREP 15 mins   COOK 20 mins

Ingredients

5 ounces blue cheese
⅔ cup cottage cheese
½ cup Greek yogurt
6 corn cobs, in their husks
salt and pepper, to taste

1. Crumble the blue cheese, then place in a bowl. Beat with a wooden spoon until creamy. Beat in the cottage cheese until thoroughly blended. Gradually beat in the yogurt and season with salt and pepper. Cover with plastic wrap and chill in the refrigerator until required. Meanwhile, preheat the oven to 425°F.

2. Fold back the husks on each corn cob and remove the silks. Smooth the husks back into place. Cut out six rectangles of aluminum foil, each large enough to enclose a corn cob. Wrap the corn cobs in the foil.

3. Place the corn cobs in the preheated oven and cook for 20 minutes. Unwrap the corn cobs and discard the foil. Peel back the husk on one side of each and trim off with a sharp knife. Serve with the blue cheese dressing.

Ketchup

MAKES
1 CUP

PREP
10 mins

COOK
20 mins

Ingredients

2 tablespoons olive oil
1 red onion, peeled and chopped
2 garlic cloves, chopped
4 plum tomatoes, diced
1 cup canned, diced tomatoes
½ teaspoon ground ginger
½ teaspoon chili powder
3 tablespoons packed dark brown sugar
½ cup red wine vinegar
salt and pepper, to taste

1. Heat the olive oil in a large saucepan and add the onion, garlic, and tomatoes. Add the ginger and chili powder and season with salt and pepper. Cook for 15 minutes, or until soft.

2. Pour the mixture into a food processor or blender and blend well. Strain thoroughly to remove all the seeds. Return the mixture to the pan and add the sugar and vinegar. Return to a boil and cook until it is the consistency of store-bought ketchup.

3. Transfer to sterilized jars, let cool completely, then seal. Store in the refrigerator and use within one month.

Barbecue Sauce

Ingredients

1 tablespoon olive oil
1 small onion,
finely chopped
2–3 garlic cloves,
crushed
1 fresh red jalapeño
chile, seeded and finely
chopped (optional)
2 teaspoons tomato paste
1 teaspoon dry mustard,
or to taste
1 tablespoon red wine
vinegar
1 tablespoon
Worcestershire sauce
2–3 teaspoons packed
dark brown sugar
1¼ cups water

1. Heat the oil in a small, heavy saucepan, add the onion, garlic, and chile, if using, and gently sauté, stirring frequently, for 3 minutes, or until beginning to soften. Remove from the heat.

2. Blend the tomato paste with the mustard, vinegar, and Worcestershire sauce to a smooth paste, then stir into the onion mixture with 2 teaspoons of the sugar. Mix well, then gradually stir in the water.

3. Return to the heat and bring to a boil, stirring frequently. Reduce the heat and gently simmer, stirring occasionally, for 15 minutes. Taste and add the remaining sugar, if desired. Serve hot or cold.

Scalloped Potatoes

Ingredients

FEEDS 4 · **PREP 10 mins** · **COOK 1½ hours**

4 large baking potatoes
oil, for brushing
2 tablespoons milk or
light cream
2 eggs, separated
1 cup shredded cheddar
cheese
1 tablespoon butter
4 scallions, finely
chopped
salt and pepper, to taste

1. Preheat the oven to 400°F. Place the potatoes on a baking sheet, brush with oil, and rub with salt. Bake in the preheated oven for 1–1¼ hours, until tender.

2. Cut a slice from the top of the potatoes and scoop out the flesh, leaving about a ¼-inch-thick shell. Put the flesh into a bowl. Add the milk, egg yolks, and half the cheese, then mash together.

3. Melt the butter in a small saucepan, add the scallions, and sauté for 1–2 minutes, until soft. Stir into the potato mixture and season with salt and pepper.

4. Beat the egg whites in a grease-free bowl until they hold soft peaks. Fold them lightly into the potato mixture, then spoon the mixture back into the shells.

5. Place the filled potatoes on the baking sheet and sprinkle the remaining cheese on top. Bake for 15–20 minutes, until golden. Serve immediately.

Baked Cauliflower

Ingredients

FEEDS 4–6 **PREP 10 mins** **COOK 30 mins**

1 head of cauliflower, trimmed and cut into florets

⅔ cup white wine

1 bay leaf

2 cups milk

2 tablespoons butter, cut into pieces

3 tablespoons all-purpose flour

⅔ cup shredded cheddar cheese

½ cup grated Parmesan cheese

1 teaspoon English mustard

1 tablespoon snipped fresh chives

1 tablespoon chopped fresh parsley

salt, to taste

1. Cook the cauliflower in a large saucepan of lightly salted boiling water for 6–8 minutes, until tender but still firm to the bite. Drain and set aside. Preheat the oven to 400°F.

2. Place the wine and bay leaf in a saucepan. Boil rapidly until the wine is reduced by half. Add the milk, butter, and flour and whisk until the butter has melted. Continue whisking until the sauce boils and thickens. Simmer for 1 minute.

3. Remove from the heat. Mix the cheeses together and stir two-thirds into the sauce until smooth, then stir in the mustard, chives, and parsley. Remove and discard the bay leaf.

4. Spoon a little of the sauce over the bottom of a shallow baking dish. Transfer the cauliflower to the dish and spread out in an even layer. Spoon the remaining sauce over the top and sprinkle with the remaining cheese. Bake in the preheated oven for 20 minutes, until lightly browned and bubbling. Serve immediately.

Wine, fresh herbs, and punchy Parmesan have been added to this modern version of the classic dish.

Coleslaw

Ingredients

FEEDS 6   **PREP 10 mins**

⅔ cup mayonnaise
(see page 107)
⅔ cup plain yogurt
dash of hot sauce
1 head of green cabbage
4 carrots
1 green bell pepper
salt and pepper, to taste

1. To make the dressing, mix together the mayonnaise, yogurt, hot sauce, and salt and pepper in a small bowl. Chill in the refrigerator until required.

2. Cut the cabbage in half and then into quarters. Remove and discard the tough stem in the center. Finely shred the cabbage leaves. Wash the leaves under cold running water and dry thoroughly on paper towels. Peel the carrots and coarsely shred in a food processor or on a mandoline. Quarter and seed the bell pepper and cut the flesh into thin strips.

3. Mix the vegetables together in a large serving bowl and toss to mix. Pour over the dressing and toss until the vegetables are well coated. Cover and chill in the refrigerator until required.

Reduce the green cabbage to ½ head, and add ½ head of red cabbage for a more colorful slaw.

New Potatoes

with garlic and chili butter

 Ingredients

 FEEDS 4

 PREP 10 mins

 COOK 20 mins

Ingredients

1½ pounds baby new potatoes
3 tablespoons butter
1 garlic clove, finely chopped
1 red chile, seeded and finely chopped
salt and pepper, to taste
chopped fresh parsley leaves, to garnish

1. Bring a large saucepan of lightly salted water to a boil, add the potatoes, bring back to a boil, and cook for 15 minutes, or until tender. Drain and set aside.

2. Melt the butter in a large saucepan, add the garlic and chile, and gently sauté for 30 seconds, without browning.

3. Add the potatoes and stir to coat in the butter, then season with salt and pepper. Sprinkle with the parsley and serve hot.

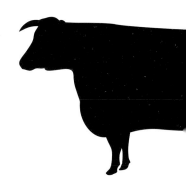